+/+

THE NATIONAL ACADEMY
presents the following examples of the Work of
EDWIN AUSTIN ABBEY N A , R. A

## CONTENTS

1   The Village Preacher
          from "The Deserted Village'
2   The Education of Isabella the Catholic
3   "The Ladies of St James's'
          by "Austen Dobson
4   Lady Ann and the Duke of Gloucester
          from "Richard the Third"
5   'Sweet Nelly, my Heart s Delight"
          from ' Old Songs
6   The Prince of Morocco, Portia and Nerissa
          from ' The Merchant of Venice
7   Play Scene in ' Hamlet '
8   A Love Song' A Love Song'
          from "Twelfth Night
9   Miss Hardcastle and Miss Neville
          from "She Stoops to Conquer
10   Trial of Queen Katherine
          from   Henry the Eighth
11   The Re-entrance of the Players
          from   Mid-summer Night s Dream
12   King Lear s Daughters
13   The Penance of Eleanor
          from   Henry the Sixth   Part II.
14   Crusader Sighting Jerusalem as the Sun Rises
15   May Morning
16   Columbus in the New World

          Harrisburg Decorations

17   Spirit of Vulcan
18   Spirit of Light
19   Science Revealing the Treasures of the Earth
20   Spirit of Religious Liberty
21   A Banqueting Room in Timon s House
          '          from   Timons of Athens
22   Mrs E A Abbey
23   The Coronation of King Edward the Seventh


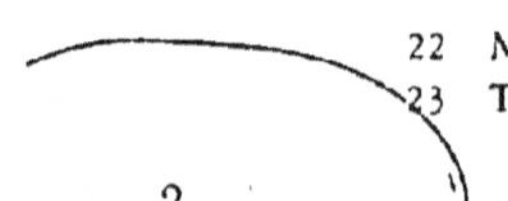

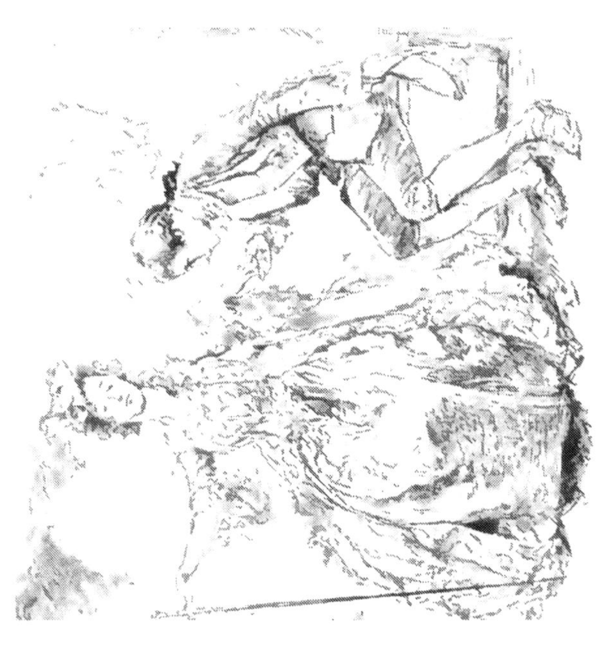

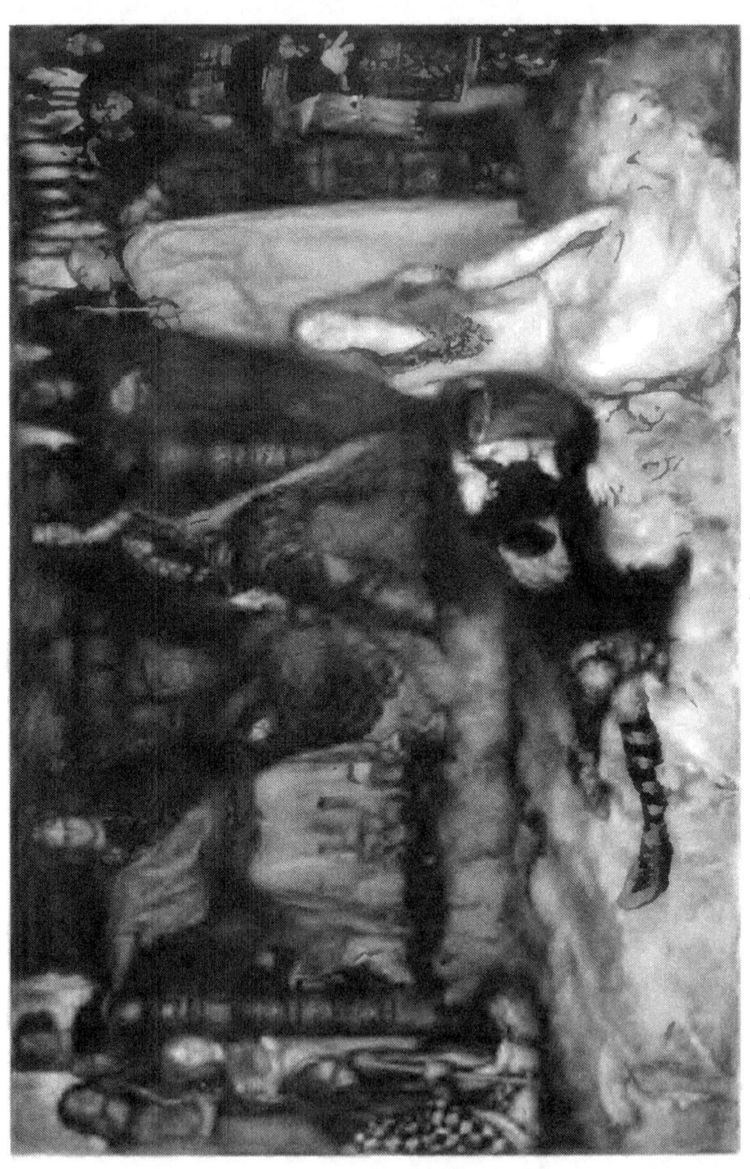

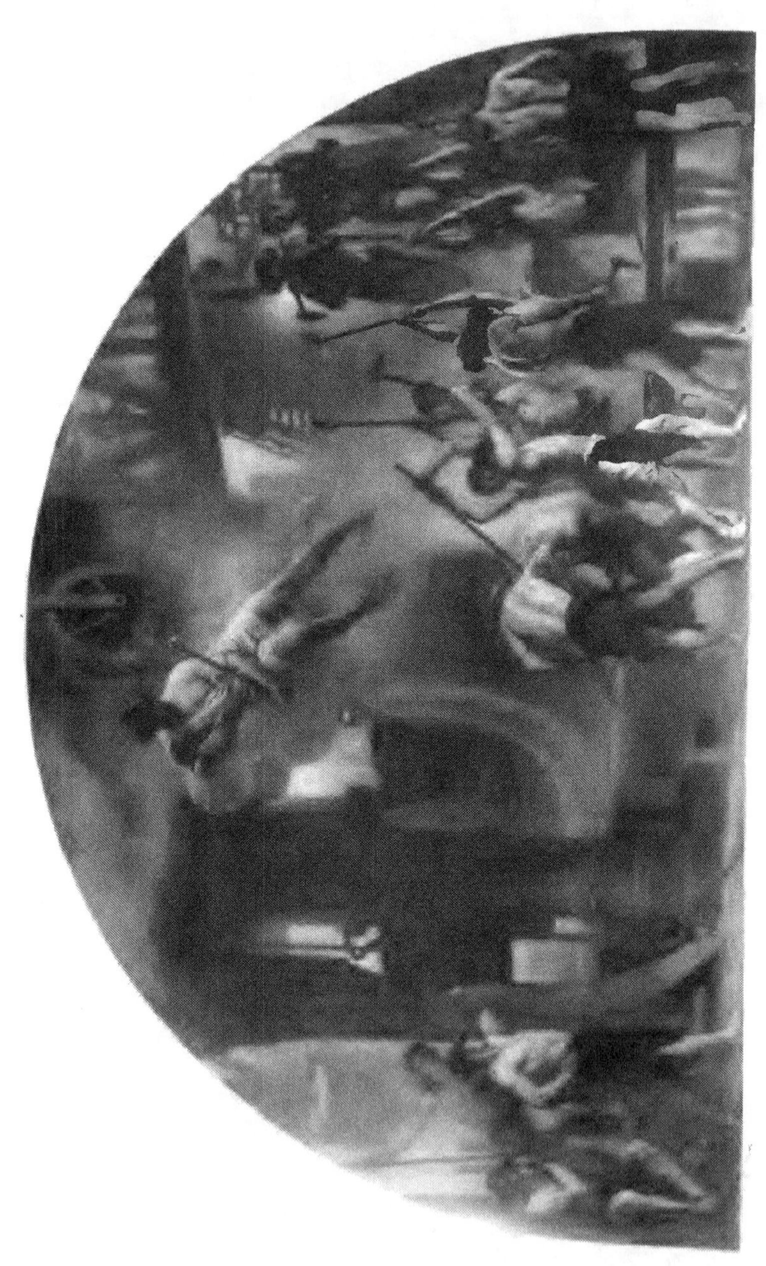

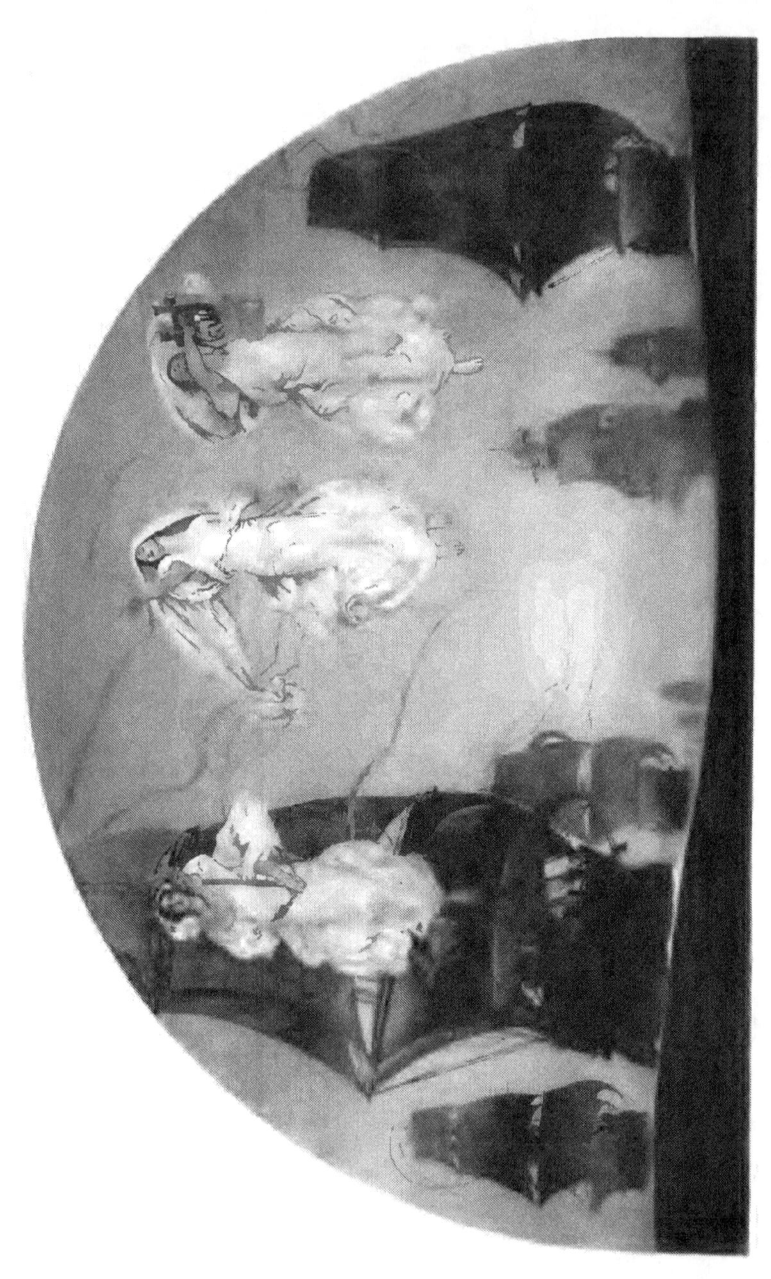

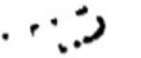

301028